The Point in the Heart
A Source of Delight for My Soul

LAITMAN
KABBALAH
PUBLISHERS

MICHAEL LAITMAN

The Point in the Heart

A Source of Delight for My Soul

The Point in the Heart
A Source of Delight for My Soul

Copyright © 2010 by Michael Laitman
All rights reserved. Published by Laitman Kabbalah Publishers
www.kabbalah.info info@kabbalah.info
1057 Steeles Avenue West, Suite 532, Toronto, ON, M2R 3X1, Canada
2009 85th Street #51, Brooklyn, New York, 11214, USA

Printed in Canada

ISBN 978-1-897448-41-0

Compiled by:	Oren Levi
Translation:	Yuval Edoot
Copy Editor:	Claire Gerus
Associate Editors:	Susan Gal, Riggan Shilston, Debra Rudder
Layout:	Rami Yaniv, Baruch Khovov
Cover Design:	Rami Yaniv, Baruch Khovov
Printing and Post Production:	Uri Laitman
Executive Editor:	Chaim Ratz

FIRST EDITION: FEBRUARY 2011
First printing

Contents

Foreword

We are living in a very special time. People all over the world are dissatisfied with their lives; they sense that life should offer so much more, and they want it.

This longing is the awakening of "the point in the heart." We all have it, and now it is beginning to emerge in millions.

* * *

EVERY section in this book is unique and thought provoking, gently and sincerely dealing with the deepest questions that concern all of us today.

In these pages you will also find tidbits from the wisdom contained in *The Book of Zohar* (the essential book in all of Kabbalah) and other Kabbalistic writings. This book does not profess to teach Kabbalah, but rather introduces selected ideas from the teachings. You are about to embark on a journey that will span the depths of the heart, and the height of thought.

The Editor

The wisdom of Kabbalah
is an advanced science.
It is a science of emotion,
a science of pleasure.
You are welcome to open and to taste.

The Point
in the Heart

The advent of the "Point in the Heart"
within us heralds the beginning
of a very special adventure,
a journey to a wonderful land

Succeed Beyond Your Dreams

Imagine for a moment that when you wake up in the morning, you suddenly know the most important law of reality—the law that defines everything.

You understand what you should or should not do to avoid all pain, unpleasantness, and suffering; everything is clear to you, and you awaken to life like a child—full of enthusiasm and without fears or inhibitions. This is precisely how we should live.

And actually, why not? Why do we sometimes fail? Why do we bump into walls, suffer blows, and face problems? Why do we need to be in darkness?

If we discover this most important law, we will have no problems; we'll know exactly how to conduct our lives and how to succeed beyond our wildest dreams.

The Upper Law

The wisdom of Kabbalah is a science that reveals the superior guidance behind the whole of creation.

The whole of reality is guided by one inclusive law, called "the law of nature" or "the law of the Creator." This is the law of all-encompassing love, harmony, and benevolence. Kabbalah gives us the opportunity to discover this law, and to lead our lives accordingly.

As it is essential to know the basic laws of physics, chemistry, and biology in order to lead a normal life, it is essential to know the wisdom of Kabbalah. Realizing the inclusive law of creation and living by it will spare us suffering, wars, and natural disasters, bringing us to a state of balance and harmony.

The general law of nature - the Creator - love and giving

Man is enslaved in all his motions,
shackled in iron chains
by the views and manners of others,
who are society

That is what the great Kabbalist, Rav Yehuda Ashlag,
known as Baal HaSulam, explains in his essay, "The Freedom"

This Marathon
Has Run Its Course

We may think we have everything, but everything no longer satisfies us.

We are still playing the game and chasing transient goals, which we envision as pleasures such as money, honors, and power. After all, what else is there to do in this life?

We look at each other and thoughtlessly follow the current trend. We say to ourselves, "If I behave like everyone else, I'll feel good." Then, we choose a certain vague, agreeable goal and chase it, hoping to escape the emptiness.

We must be constantly preoccupied or the eternal questions will haunt us: "What am I living for? What's happening with my life?"

But sooner or later, the point in our hearts will awaken and we will not be able to focus on mundane issues.

Suddenly, we will understand that this chase was prearranged in order to distract our minds from what is most important.

As long as we closed our eyes to avoid truly seeing, we could run along with the crowd.

But we have exhausted our strength. While everyone else is still racing, we have dropped out. It is simply not appealing anymore; in fact, we find it pointless.

Our will has deepened so much, it no longer allows us to settle for mundane goals. This is when we begin the quest for a higher goal.

*"The Light of Klipot" (Shells)
is when it seems to us
that if we had a million dollars
we would be happy*

The Thread to Love

Once, or several times in life,
in each of us,
a point in the heart awakens.

At times it feels like you are empty,
at times you feel
unhappy for no apparent reason.

At other times it is
for seemingly mundane,
worldly reasons, even familial.

You think, "It'll pass;
the storm will calm
and all will be well again."

You may not realize it,
but this is how the point in the heart is
awakened in you.

It is the beginning of the soul,
the first step toward
revealing love.

A Package for You

When a certain thought about the meaning of life awakens in us, it is a sign that the Creator has invited us to contact Him, to touch base.

It is as if a courier were knocking on our door saying, "A package for you!"—This is how the invitation arrives.

We must open the door, accept the package, open it, and from its content recognize its sender and how we should respond to it.

We hear the knocking on the door but we wait, sitting on the couch, too idle to get up. We yell to the courier, "Leave it by the door; I'll pick it up later."

This attitude causes the awakening to dissipate, and who knows when will be the next time that we feel a knock on the door of our heart?

When we receive an invitation, we should promptly realize it and go all out to discover what is in the package, find the Sender's address, and knock on His door.

Revealing the Creator - Revealing the Spiritual World
↘ Within Us ↗

Here and Now

You cannot take a train ride
to the spiritual world;
you cannot fly there, either,
because it is *within us*.

We need only evoke
the spiritual sensation within us,
sharpen our senses,
and open wide our perception
to what is happening right here.

Then we will find ourselves in a never-ending,
wonderful adventure
that will leave us agape with awe.

And from then on,
it will never stop growing.

The Human Ego

When I look at others,
My ego evokes envy and hate
and desire to control.

I don't wish others well,
or at least, not better than me.

I want them to succeed a little,
a relative success,
but I want everyone to see that I am more successful.

Time to Break Free

Our nature, through which we sense the world and ourselves alive and operating in it, is a program that depicts a certain reality for us.

It is called "Ego"—the will to receive and to enjoy by myself and for myself, even when it is at the expense of others.

This software locks us from within, immerses us within it, draws all of our attention, and actually compels us to focus solely on ourselves.

We operate according to this program and cannot even contemplate the existence of another reality.

Ego - Human Nature – The Will to Receive

We must not destroy anything within us.
Even the most negative attributes
should remain.
We do not create anything new,
but only correct how we use
what already exists within us.

Contrasts

QUESTION: Why were we created with ego in the first place, if we will eventually have to correct it?

We come to know the world by comparing opposites— hot vs. cold, black vs. white. We recognize one in relation to the other. If everything were white, we wouldn't detect anything. Likewise, if everything were black, we wouldn't detect anything, either.

Contrast is always necessary, the disparity between colors, sensations, and places. We sense the differences between things, but not each thing separately.

The Creator is love and bestowal. However, we will not be able to sense what bestowal is if we are not opposite to it. This is why we need the ego—"help made against him." Being opposite from the Creator helps us know and sense the Creator.

The Creator—the desire to love and give

The creature—the desire to receive

↓

**Because we are currently
opposite from the Creator
we are hiding Him from ourselves**

↓

**Correction—as we acquire
the quality of love and bestowal
we equalize with the Creator
and begin to sense Him**

Love
means to regard the other as yourself.
You know the other's desires.
You sense them as your own desires,
and you do everything you can to satisfy them

Emerging into a Reality of Love

QUESTION: People around me want nothing but to hurt me! What do we do when one tries to love and the other does not?

The mutual love that we aspire for is impossible within the ego. I "love" another person because he is good for me, but in fact, I want only to exploit him.

Love within the ego is like loving fish—I love fish because I enjoy them. In the same manner, as long as I enjoy someone I enjoy being with him and I "love" him. But the moment I don't enjoy being with him, I push him away.

But there is another love, one which we still don't know. It exists above our selfish considerations, above our nature. When the picture of us being parts of a single, inclusive, and interdependent system is revealed to us, we surrender to its power and the true love of others awakens within us.

And beyond this love there is an even higher love. Beyond mutual dependency, the quality of love itself is drawing us towards it, for we realize that loving and bestowing are the most exalted things in reality.

Love allows us to transcend our regular perception and begin to sense another reality.

When our natural aspiration to absorb everything within us changes into the aspiration to love and to give, the minute and limited reality we now sense relinquishes its place, and the complete reality appears to us—the spiritual reality.

One who comes to feel the spiritual reality realizes that people mistreat each other because they are naturally controlled by the ego, not because they are evil. He discovers that they were deliberately created that way to eventually attain independent awareness of the nullity of the ego. Only then will they emerge from it into a reality of love.

A Social Network
on the Spiritual Level

QUESTION: It seems to me that people prefer to communicate by e-mails and SMS instead of speaking to each other. Why is it so?

Today the ego has evolved to such a degree that we prefer a more virtual relationship with others.

It is not that we do or do not want others. But we feel better, more comfortable, more complete when we connect with others through text messages or a computer screen, or something else.

Why? Because in this way we don't touch others' bodies, their external forms.

To understand why it happens, we must know the root of this phenomenon. The desire to receive in us has evolved and wishes to transcend the animal level of our bodies. The animal level has nothing further to give us; it does not provide us contact with others. However, we do seek deeper contact with others, so for the time being we turn to virtual relationships.

In the next phase, virtual relationships will not satisfy us and we will want an even deeper connection. Amidst the virtual connection, we will sense a need to be internally, spiritually connected with others.

The more removed we become on the physical level, the more we sense the need for connection. This explains the revolution of the internet and why everyone is so drawn to it.

Where does this attraction come from, which sometimes turns into an actual obsession? It comes from our wish to satisfy our need for connection with others. Although social networks and forums today are usually filled with drivel, and surely there is no true fulfillment in this connection, there is nevertheless a kind of connection here and it addicts us.

*As children, we all ask questions
that relate to the meaning of life,
to the connection with the Creator.
These are the most natural questions
that one asks oneself.
But then we stifle them within us
and live like robots.*

There Is None Else Besides Him

Imagine being a newborn baby,
your first sensation
that someone is caring for you.

A feeling that there is someone huge,
who shows his warm, caring,
and benevolent feelings toward you.

You cannot understand him yet,
but you know that he takes care of you,
does everything that is good for you,
and you are completely under his control.

Thus, gradually, people will come to feel
the caring and overseeing influence
of the Upper Force,
the only force in the world.

The Creator—Come and See

Various religions depict the Creator as something outside of us. But Kabbalah explains that it is forbidden to imagine the Creator as an image of any kind, that the Creator is a quality that exists within each of us.

The Creator is the quality of love and bestowal. The meaning of the word "Creator" (*Borre* in Hebrew) is "Come and See" (*Bo u Re'e*), meaning come and discover this quality within you.

There is no external, foreign element for whom we work! We work on correcting ourselves, on attaining the qualities of love and giving, the Creator.

Around two thousand years ago, we lost the feeling of the Creator—we were exiled and lost the true picture of the world. We began to think that the Creator was someone who existed separately from us, rather than a quality that appeared within us.

Instead of depicting the Creator as the primary and foremost quality of Creation, which clothes within us, we began to think of Him as a separate and foreign entity.

Focus on the Creator

The wisdom of Kabbalah teaches a person
how to turn oneself from within
and find the Creator.

It is like searching for an object
through a lens of a camera,
turning right and left,
gradually sharpening the vision
until suddenly, viola!

We see clearly.

Regaining Awareness

QUESTION: Why isn't the Creator happy when a person enjoys his corporeal life and feels satisfied?

It doesn't make the Creator happy because it is not the pleasure He intended to give us. Initially, He created a state where we were filled with light, but now we are not feeling it.

We are in an infinite, eternal world, but it is hidden from us. We are like an unconscious person who is really in this world, yet his senses perceive nothing of his surroundings.

The Creator cannot leave us unconscious, with merely a spark of light given to us only to somehow sustain us.

We are unaware of it, and we are willing to settle for the pleasures we experience at present. Nevertheless, it is clear that the plan of the Creator—to lead us to far greater pleasure—cannot remain unfulfilled.

A Field of Love

The Creator is a spiritual field of love and bestowal. We move within in it by shifting our desires, while constantly being at the point of resemblance to this field.

Initially, we are opposite from the field; we are in its outermost circle, called "This World."

To the extent of our level of desire to draw nearer to the center, to the quality of the Creator of love and bestowal, we evoke the influence of this field upon us, and it shifts our position.

Accordingly, it is clear that we cannot ask the Creator to change His attitude toward us or hope for any special favors on His part. It is as pointless as asking gravity not to affect our bodies.

The Creator is a force that is inconsiderate of our words, but considers instead our innermost desires.

The wisdom of Kabbalah teaches the laws of the spiritual world; it is spiritual physics.

"Above"
in nature
there is a force
that responds
only to one's request
to become loving and giving

The Point and the Light

QUESTION: Is it possible to point to an inner compass that guides us in our spiritual development?

To prepare us for spiritual development, nature awakens two sensations within us. The first is that this world is empty, and the second is a yearning to attain the origin of life, the awakening of the point in the heart.

Because our world is a spiritual field, just like a magnetic field, this point will lead us to a place where we can nourish it, fulfill it.

We should advance on our spiritual path only from within this point. We should neither believe anyone nor be influenced by any "words of wisdom" that we may be told. Rather, we should check everything out for ourselves; this is how we discern our way.

This scrutiny is fuelled by our demand to know the truth. We must not agree to be told, "First you must do... and then... there are conditions..."—there aren't any!

When the spiritual world is revealed
we discover a treasure,
or more precisely, "a deposit,"
a new layer of reality
that has been in our "account"
from the beginning

A World of Warmth

There are moments when feelings of excitement and elation suddenly envelop us.

We feel that the world around us is imbued with a certain force, that the air has grown "thick," filled with a new entity, that all around are thoughts and intentions directed toward us, that everything is filled with love.

It seldom happens. But what is important is that in the end a distinct sensation will remain in the heart. This is the spiritual world, to the extent that we attain it.

The spiritual world is an eternal realm whose power is enormous. One who elevates even to the first, smallest spiritual degree experiences a spiritual sensation that is a billion times greater than anything previously known.

Spiritual Waves

Our inner work
is to fine-tune our hearts and senses
to perceive the spiritual world.

Like a radio receiver
detecting air waves
as the buttons are gently turned.

Thus one tunes oneself
becoming more and more attuned
to the spiritual frequency
through actions called "intent."

Until a new dimension suddenly opens
and the spiritual world appears.

Intention Is the Deed

Intention is our only action; other actions are simply nonexistent. It is not only our mechanical actions—even our desires do not really exist. Everything is motionless, lifeless, standing still as if planted in the ground—all but the intent.

In the spiritual world, only our intentions for love and bestowal take root.

When they appear within us, we appear in the spiritual world. When they disappear, we disappear from the spiritual world.

It is similar to acceleration as the derivative of motion. As Albert Einstein determined, movement at a fixed, unchanging velocity is considered rest; hence, only acceleration should be taken into consideration.

Pleasures, Lights, and Vessels

QUESTION: Why are people so drawn to sex?

In the spiritual world the soul is in a state of "coupling" with the Light. This is the merging of both parts of Creation—the feminine part and the masculine part—and it induces the most intense sensation of pleasure in reality: the filling of the soul with Light.

The projection of the spiritual coupling in the corporeal world is physical coupling. This is also the reason why sex is considered the root of all desires in our world, and why we are so preoccupied with it.

Sexual pleasure in our world exemplifies the difference between corporeal pleasure and spiritual pleasure. One may think about sex so much and anxiously anticipate the great pleasure, but at the climax, the very moment of release, the pleasure dissipates and almost instantly dissolves. And the race begins anew, in search of the next pleasure...

Why? Because the Light extinguishes the vessel, meaning a pleasure that directly satisfies a desire neutralizes the feeling of pleasure just like plus and minus.

So now what? Now we have doubled emptiness. This is why we are told, "One does not leave this world with half one's desires in one's hand."

Spiritual pleasure works differently. To "be in spirituality" means to have a *Masach* (in Hebrew: "Screen"),the ability to receive Light inside the vessel with an aspiration to bring pleasure to the Creator, the Giver of the Light. To do that, we must acquire the Creator's quality of love and bestowal.

What do we get out of it? Spiritual coupling, a never-ending coupling that intensifies in time, yielding a feeling of eternal life. Actually, subconsciously, from the depths of our souls, we aspire only for this coupling, as this is the purpose of our being.

Why Is It So Important for Women to Be Beautiful?

QUESTION: Why are women so preoccupied with their appearance? What is the root of the importance of a woman's appearance in her own eyes and in the eyes of men?

Women's tendency to adorn themselves stems from a very high root. In spirituality, to adorn oneself means to correct oneself in accord with the Creator, the force of love and bestowal.

This inclination is rooted deep within our souls. Within us exists the point in the heart, which awakens us to adorn our "ugly" egoistic nature, to beautify it.

Being beautiful means being like the Creator. A person becomes beautiful when the Light of the Creator shines in him.

So why do women adorn themselves? In our world, women represent *Malchut* (Hebrew: "Kingship"), the root of Creation. A man and a woman, or groom and bride, represent the relationship between the Creator and the creature—the creature being a woman, and the Creator being a man.

Thus, each of us, women and men alike, needs to learn to adorn the soul and become beautiful!

The Method
of Correction

Surrounding Light

Gradually, we are coming to realize that as long as the ego rules, the end of the world is nearing and we must choose life and love. But without help, we will not be able to transcend our egos because it is how we were born. To do that, we need an outside force that does not exist in our world. This is why we were given a correction method—Kabbalah.

There is a special force in the wisdom of Kabbalah, one that can create a new quality within us. Kabbalah describes the nature of the Creator, the upper world and the processes that occur therein. When we learn about these processes, about actions of love and bestowal, we draw the force from them toward us.

This projection of the upper states on our current state is called "the action of the reforming light," the "surrounding light." Eventually, the surrounding light makes us yearn for the quality of the Creator.

Baal HaSulam explains it in the following manner: "Through the yearning and the great desire to understand what they are learning, they awaken upon themselves the lights that surround their souls ... which bring one much closer to achieving perfection."

("Introduction to the Study of the Ten Sefirot", Item 155)

A Request to Achieve Completeness

QUESTION: How can the action of the surrounding light, the "Light that Reforms," be explained in simple words?

Nature, the Upper Force, the force of love and bestowal, exists in the bonding of all the parts of Creation—which He Himself created—and they exist in harmony and a totally reciprocal connection.

We are unhappy because we have become detached from this integral system. If we want to be happy, we should return to this system, which is called "perfection."

How can we return? When we want and make an effort to return to the system, we evoke a force within it, which affects us. Thus, we awaken upon us the "surrounding light," the "Light that Reforms," a force that leads us back into the general system.

This force acts in congruence with the power of our will—the extent to which we awaken, request, and even demand it from the system.

From Evolution's Steam Engine to Spirituality's Jet Engine

Who can explain how an infant grows into an adult? Why do babies change from day to day? Science can describe what unfolds within matter, but it does not see the cause that exists *outside of* matter, driving it to develop.

I left science decades ago because that was exactly what I wanted to know—where does the force of life come from? Where can it be found? In atoms? In molecules? In systems within the cells? I discovered that science does not research that. But if we do not know the answer to the most important issue or even try to discover it, then what is the point of science?

According to Kabbalah, the same force that acts upon and develops every part of Creation acts upon the infant, too. It is the light of life, the Upper Force, which operates in creation and turns inanimate matter into plants, animals, and humans. Without it, matter would remain lifeless and unchanging.

The light of life cannot be perceived or measured with any instrument. We see only the effects of its operation, such as an infant who grows from day to day and from moment to moment. In our world, this light creates evolution.

But the train of evolution lags along at its own pace as the Upper Force operates in matter and drives it to its predetermined goal.

When we enter the spiritual world, we can research every stage of evolution, even the dinosaur era, should that suddenly interest you, since all of the previous forms are known in advance and must clothe their forms according to the different combinations of the forces of reception and bestowal.

The wisdom of Kabbalah describes the future states of our development. When we study it with a desire to develop, we consciously draw the light of life to act upon us. In such a case, the effect of the light upon us is defined as the act of the surrounding light. Today the possibility to do so is open to all of us.

The Book of Zohar is a river
emerging from the Garden of Eden
flowing through one's heart.

* * *

Without The Book of Zohar
we would not be able to focus
on the inner, spiritual world.
We would always see the superficial picture,
the picture of the corporeal world,
the world of outcomes.

The Book of Zohar—
Inlet to the Hidden World

The most prominent book in the wisdom of Kabbalah is *The Book of Zohar*. It was written by a group of ten great Kabbalists, a group unparalleled in history.

They created a bridge of language, information, and feelings, forces, and lights between the way we understand and feel the revealed world, and our understanding of the hidden world.

When we study *The Book of Zohar* and try to experience the state that the Kabbalists are trying to convey to us, we are as wide-eyed babies opening our mouths and passionately absorbing our mothers' words. We do not understand them, but we look at them and express our joy with movements.

From within us, from an unknown layer in our subconscious, a new space will begin to appear, a new world to which we will gradually become accustomed. Thus, that which was concealed will slowly become revealed.

Actually, *The Zohar* is not "studied," it is *revealed* through our yearning, through our willingness to feel the hidden world.

It is for good reason that whenever Kabbalists write about *The Book of Zohar* they do not use the expression, *The Book of Zohar*, but only "The Book."

In doing so, they show us that there is no other book in the world!

The uniqueness of The Book of Zohar
is in its ability
to take any person who so desires,
whomever he is and wherever he may be,
and admit him into the spiritual world.

Acquaintance with Myself

QUESTION: I happened to watch a lesson you gave to your students on *The Book of Zohar* and other Kabbalah writings. I did not understand much, but I felt that there was something special there. Is there any point in watching lessons even without understanding?

Absolutely. Watching these lessons awakens the effect of the surrounding light on you, even without your cognitive understanding of the material being studied. It is said about it, "The heart understands."

In general, when studying *The Book of Zohar* we come across many things that are not clear to us. We gradually become acquainted with them, but actually, it is not even that important.

We can compare this process to a small child who sees many new and unfamiliar things around him. While he does not know why they are needed, in this way, without understanding how, he comes to know the world in an instinctive, pure, and innocent way.

There is no need to fear not understanding the material or not knowing how one thing relates to another. We simply need to listen, touch everything, burn from within, and want to understand. This is the only way to come to know the world, our world and the spiritual world.

The Book of Zohar and all the writings of Kabbalah turn to the internal forces within us. They help us gradually become acquainted with them. As we evolve, we get more opportunities to work with these forces, to rearrange them, and to use them properly.

Light of Hassadim (Mercy) in the Midst of a Sea of Light of Hochma (Wisdom)

We are in a fixed state called *Ein Sof* (Infinity). The Creator desires to fill us boundlessly, that we will understand and feel "from the end of the world to its end." The problem is that we are obtuse. We lack the sense with which we can perceive the whole of reality.

We have a body that is a kind of inclusive sense. Within it are five particular senses through which we sense only this world.

But there is another sense that we do not presently feel. It is called "a soul." In it are five particular senses, too, called *Keter, Hochma, Bina, Tifferet,* and *Malchut.* When we reveal our soul, we will sense the spiritual world through it.

There is only one thing that we lack in order to reveal our souls, to feel that even now we are in the world of *Ein Sof,* that everything shines around us, and there are no limits—the light of *Hassadim* (mercy). The light of *Hassadim* is love, bestowal, and rising above the ego.

In Kabbalistic terms, we are currently in a sea of light of *Hochma* (wisdom), but we can reveal it only to the extent that we open ourselves with the light of *Hassadim.*

If there is any pressure from the light of *Hochma*, and there is no light of *Hassadim* on the soul's part with which to open itself and to shine, darkness ensues.

The point in the heart within us is like a drop of "the semen of the soul." Studying Kabbalah brings the surrounding light to it and gradually builds the light of *Hassadim* in it. Thus, the soul evolves and fills with the light of *Hochma*.

Endless Pleasure

The wisdom of Kabbalah deals with receiving all the abundance that is intended for us (in Hebrew, Kabbalah means "receiving"). It explains how to receive and transfer immense and eternal pleasure through ourselves.

Eternal—because when we transfer the fulfillment of all the souls through ourselves, we are not depleted. It is like a mother who loves all of her children and enjoys the gifts that she transfers to all of them.

The Goal of Creation
Is to Enjoy

QUESTION: I still do not understand what am I going to get out of loving others.

Loving others is not the goal; it is the means. The goal of Creation is to enjoy! But to truly enjoy, "large vessels" are required, receptacles, great desires for pleasure, so they can be filled with abundance.

I was born with a very small vessel, tiny. I eat a little, stop, and want no more. I run to another physical pleasure, enjoy it, and that is the end of it. I go to watch something and it's over... I cannot receive any greater pleasure than what I receive now.

When I hear that the goal of Creation is to enjoy, what can I possibly imagine? To be served a 1000-pound steak? To be given such great pleasure that I will explode? My vessel cannot contain it. What can I do?

Those who have already been through this process explain that it is impossible to obtain more pleasure in the way my vessel currently obtains it. But if I expand it, I will be able to obtain more.

Don't Guess, Control Destiny!

A person does not know
what will happen to him in a moment.
It is difficult to accept this situation.

But I want more than to know the future,
I want to govern it.

I don't need fortune tellers
but a higher spiritual instrument
to indicate my future form to me.

The Desire that Switches On the Light

Darkness is lack of connection with others.

Like an electrical circuit,
whose elements are disconnected,
preventing conduction of current.

If we truly desire to connect,
that desire will switch on the light.

Shame—the Engine of Development

To avoid feeling ashamed, we must constantly adapt to codes of behavior.

Everything we do in our world, other than providing for essentials, is driven only by our need to avoid embarrassment.

Why is it so? This stems from an ancient root, from the beginning of Creation, long preceding the formation of our world and everything in it.

The Creator (the desire to bestow) created the creature (the desire to receive) and filled it with light (pleasure). After the creature enjoyed the light, it realized that there was a higher element filling it with this light, and that caused it to feel shame. Shame is the first reaction of the creature to its sensation of the Creator; hence, it is the only thing that we must complement in order to equalize with the Creator.

That is also the reason why in our world, which is an outcome of the Upper World, the sensation of shame in all its forms governs our every action.

Why Do We Feel Lonely
(even when we are surrounded by many people)?

Loneliness exists
so we may feel the need
for true connection and bonding
With all other people
and with the Creator
who will then fill us with Light.

Thoughts about Pain

Pain is the body's reaction to various bodily disruptions. Pain warns of danger, forces us to take action—to move closer or farther, to find the cause of the pain, to draw conclusions and to move on to new states.

Pain is a force that affects our ego.

There is pain because I feel bad, because others feel bad, or because others feel good.

Pain "pushes" from behind and forces us to evolve.

Pain that stems from feeling empty pulls us forward to fulfillment.

All feelings stem from conflict, contact, and pressure—from pain.

Pleasure can be felt only after feeling pain, suffering or anticipation.

We overcome pain only when we rise above the ego. All of a sudden, we realize that we can exist without lack, but with complete fulfillment, which is not based on pain. It is fulfillment does not stem from a need, but from completeness, from love.

The Light that Will Never Go Out

When we reach the middle of our lives, we start to dwindle, to gradually die out.

But it is not our body that is dying; it is our desire fading and losing its strength to push forward.

However, if we begin to develop spiritually, we receive vigor and desire to advance, like children—always wanting, constantly revitalizing.

Towards True Fear

Whoever opens *The Book of Zohar* finds that the first correction we must carry out is to obtain true fear.

People usually experience two types of fear: of this world (health, wealth, children, etc.) or of the next world (preparing themselves for heaven rather than hell).

The process of spiritual development introduces us to a third type of fear—the true fear—whether or not we will succeed in resembling the Creator and attain the quality of love and bestowal toward others and toward Him.

The study of Kabbalah develops within us the perception of the unity of everything and shifts the corporeal fears to true fear.

Pride

QUESTION: What do we do when couples turn their backs to each other and neither is able to reconcile?

Pride is the greatest and the ultimate state of the ego. We cannot swallow our pride because we feel that it eliminates us, revokes our uniqueness

However, this can change if we instill a third element into the dual configuration. The third element is the Creator. In that regard, it has been said, "A man and a woman: if they merit, Divinity is between them. If they did not merit, fire consumes them."

How is that done? We need not eliminate pride, ego, disagreements, and differences. Also, we need not try to understand each other and make peace. If we settle for these, it will merely be psychology, which will explode in our faces the next time around.

Instead, we create a triangle: You are different, in disagreement, and each carries his or her pride. But you have a mutual *higher* goal—the revelation of the Creator. And in that goal you can bond.

The Thought
Is the Servant of Desire

The Creator created a desire to receive, to enjoy, and nothing else. The greater desire to enjoy rules the smaller desire to enjoy.

If so, what are thoughts, intellect? Thoughts help us shift from one desire to another, from one state to another, from a specific form of desire to a different form of desire.

The desire is the substance of creation, and the thought is the means that helps us use these desires, to integrate them in us, to move in the force field of these desires from greater desire to a smaller one or vice versa, like moving toward a magnet or away from it.

But whatever my desire is at the moment, it always controls me.

This is why I must use the power of thought to help me understand and convince myself that my desire, my state, my current circumstances are bad, and that better circumstances exist.

In the wisdom of Kabbalah, analyzing my current desire using the thought is called "recognition of evil," and the thought develops in me by the action of the upper light.

Mind and heart alternate dominance within us, but we always move by the same flow pattern: desire-thought-desire.

Forever Young

Kabbalah deals with the soul.
This is the only organ that does not age.
The more you engage in it,
the younger you become!

It is so much so,
that at times
you even feel uncomfortable with others.
You look and behave inquisitively
when everyone around is so serious,
so full of themselves, conservative,
and you—an eternal child, forever young.

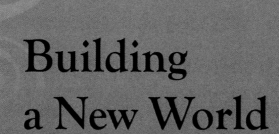

Building
a New World

When will things finally be good here?

When each of us thinks
not only of himself
but of everyone

Therefore Choose Life

Many people turn to me with concerns about the future. Our future depends on understanding what is taking place. When we understand the thought of creation, we will find that we are happy, confident, and whole.

We did not really have free will until the 21st century. We developed in a coercive, automated manner, alongside the constant heightening of egoistic drives.

Now that the human ego has culminated, an opportunity for freedom of choice arises. Now we can rise above our egoistic nature, and cease being dependent on it.

If we realize this opportunity, we will rise directly (and least painfully) to another nature, another dimension of reality, another sensation of life—in the entire volume of reality, in eternity and perfection.

Nature's plan will be executed whether or not we choose the path of conscious transition to the upper dimension, just as it has until today. However, without our participation, it will come alongside the harsh impact of the "press of evolution" upon us.

We are the only intelligent creatures in the world, and everything was created for us, as we are the only ones who can emerge into a higher dimension.

The task is serious; the goal is wonderful. The current state of humanity requires searching; hence, it is a good situation. For this reason, I do not relate to it with anxiety, but rather with much hope.

Building a World

We let our children
play with Lego, assemble puzzles, and solve problems
in short, create.
This is how they learn.

The Creator created Creation as perfect.
However, to give us a chance to grow to His level,
He completely shredded it,
down to the state of our world,
so we would recreate that perfect state.

From Separate Souls to Unity

Only in the harmonious connection
of the body parts
was healthy life created.

Within the correct bonding among people
reveals the connection
where the upper life is hidden,
the feeling of eternity and wholeness.

The impasse we have reached today
highlights the need for a transition
from the stage where souls are separated by the ego
to the stage of unity
where we reveal the upper life.

"Love your neighbor as yourself"
is the law of nature
as nature is a living body
where all parts are interconnected

Ecology—A Shift of Perception

All of our problems stem from our view of ourselves as separate from nature, distinguishing man from his environment.

Such perception of nature makes us regard all that surrounds us as subordinate to man. Even when we care for the environment, it is only for our own pleasure and not out of consideration for the whole system of nature.

Violating the balance of the closed system of nature evokes a negative feedback. And since we are an outcome of nature, we suffer on all levels of our existence.

Therefore, we must change our approach from a perception of "protecting the environment" to a perception of "man as an integral part of nature."

According to Kabbalah, our thoughts and desires are the strongest forces in reality, and are the primary cause of all the changes in nature.

The problem is that the impact of our thoughts on nature is concealed from us.

As a result, we measure only our external impact, such as gas emissions and waste pollution, while the internal cause still awaits treatment at the root.

It is well worth our while to acknowledge
that protecting the environment
primarily entails protecting ourselves
from our own egos.
And the sooner the better.

Global Hunger Is Not a Must

Our planet can feed
an unlimited number of people,
if they do not get in its way,
and if they bond
throughout the planet
as organs of a complete body.

The Creation of the World

QUESTION: How does Kabbalah relate to the contradiction between the creation of the world 5,770 years ago and the time of the "Big Bang"?

The Big Bang occurred approximately 14 billion years ago. Its cause was a spark of the upper light that reached its lowest level—egoism. The spark contained within it all the matter and energy of our world, and from it the entire universe was created.

Planet Earth was created approximately 4.6 billion years ago as a result of the condensation of the solar system. In time, the crust of the Earth cooled, the atmosphere was formed and life began. None of it was coincidental. Everything that happens is a manifestation of information that preexisted in the initial spark of light.

Following the inanimate nature, plants appeared, then animals, and finally man. The interpretation of evolution based on its superficial appearance—that species evolve from other species, which then evolve into even more species—is incorrect.

The reason for the appearance of every detail in nature is the information that was initially rooted in the spark of light. Kabbalah explains evolution as a process of unfolding bits of data (genes), called *Reshimot* (recollections).

Man developed from the ape hundreds of thousands of years ago, as the ARI (Isaac Luria) writes in *The Tree of Life*. However, only 5,770 years ago (as of the writing of this book) was a point in the heart first awakened in a human being. His name was Adam, from the verse *Adame la'Elion* ("I shall be like the Most High" Isaiah, 14:14). His name reflected his desire to resemble the Creator.

The day Adam revealed the spiritual world is called "the day of Creation." This was when humanity first touched the spiritual world, which is why it is the point from which the Hebrew count of years begins. According to the plan of Creation, within 6,000 years we must all attain the level of the Creator. This will be called "the end of correction" (of the human ego).

Small Village, Global Ego

Throughout the history of humanity, there was only one period in which the wisdom of Kabbalah was available to all. It was in ancient Babylon, a city that functioned like a small village, where every individual could influence the lives of everyone else. Society in Babylon existed as a single system, hence the need for the wisdom of Kabbalah, which teaches how to implement the law of "Love thy neighbor as thyself."

Abraham the Patriarch, a native of Babylon, called for the implementation of this law, but only a few listened to him. Only those in whom the point in the heart had revealed followed him and employed the wisdom of Kabbalah. Reflecting their deepest desire, they called themselves "Israel," from the words, *Yashar El* (straight to God), meaning directly to the quality of the Creator.

All the others in Babylon preferred not to unite, but to remain distant from each other. They scattered over the face of the Earth, and generation by generation they pursued the drives that the ego naturally aroused in them.

Abraham's group grew and developed to the size of a nation: the nation of Israel. But 2,000 years ago, a huge ego suddenly appeared within us and we fell from the degree of love of others to unfounded hatred. We lost the feeling of life as a unified system, the encompassing feeling of love disappeared, and the Creator was concealed from us. Only a few with unique qualities were drawn to revealing the Creator, engaged with the wisdom, and developed it from generation to generation, waiting for the time when all would need it.

Recently, the circle began to close and the two routes that separated in Babylon are merging. Again, the world is becoming a small village, and again, we are egoists. But now there is nowhere to run. We have become so interdependent that we are compelled to implement the law, "Love thy neighbor as thyself."

The wisdom of Kabbalah teaches how to attain the love of others in order to survive. Today, it is being revealed to everyone once more to teach us how to thrive in the new world.

True Kabbalah

The wisdom of Kabbalah was hidden for thousands of years, providing fertile ground for the springing of diverse theories as to its essence. All of them were incorrect. Today, the study of authentic Kabbalah is open to all, without any restrictions or prerequisites. However, it is important to know that the wisdom of Kabbalah engages only with man's correction.

"This wisdom is no more and no less than a sequence of roots, which hang down by way of cause and consequence, by fixed, determined rules, interweaving to a single, exalted goal described as "the revelation of His Godliness to His creatures in this world. ... the whole of humanity is obligated to eventually come to this immense evolvement."

(Baal HaSulam, "The Essence of the Wisdom of Kabbalah")

A Ladder to Infinity

The wisdom of Kabbalah teaches us that we live in a multi-layered reality.

Reality is divided into two basic levels—our world and the upper, concealed world.

The upper world consists of 125 different degrees of existence positioned one atop the other, like a ladder with 125 rungs.

At present, we exist below even the lowest rung on the ladder. The point in the heart evokes us to climb up to its first rung.

When we discover that there is a higher rung, the urge to reach it and climb up the ladder will awaken in us until we reach its top.

This form of development will lead us to infinity.

The Wisdom of the Hidden

We research our world through science and discover that which is concealed from us.

The knowledge that science accumulates helps us in this world. Even if we know nothing from our own life experience, we trust scientists, physicians, and other experts. Although science has not yet discovered everything about our world, with time, more of the concealed becomes revealed.

Yet, there is another part to reality, a concealed world, a higher world that science cannot discover. To be able to sense this part of reality, one must correct one's nature, the ego, and acquire the quality of love and bestowal. Only then does one begin to sense the concealed world and study it scientifically.

The different belief systems and religions are theories regarding the hidden world (God) and the things this world compels us to do. These theories are diverse, often contradictory, and exist precisely because that part of reality is concealed from us. However, none of them provides practical recommendations for revealing the concealed world (revealing God).

Kabbalists are people who have acquired the quality of love and bestowal, through which they have attained the concealed world. They describe the structure of the upper world and offer the opportunity to reveal it to anyone who is interested. We are not required to change our ways of life, since there is no connection between corporeal actions and the acquisition of the quality of love and bestowal. Kabbalah is not about believing in Divinity, but about *revealing* it.

The Indignant Question

The fundamental textbook with which we study the wisdom of Kabbalah is *The Study of the Ten Sefirot.* In this book, Baal HaSulam interprets the words of the ARI (Isaac Luria), which are vital for the development of the souls in our generation.

Baal HaSulam opens the preface to the book by introducing different doubts people have regarding the study of Kabbalah. He does not refer to these doubts directly, but rather turns elsewhere, to the question regarding the meaning of life:

"Indeed, if we set our hearts to answer but one very famous question, I am certain that all these questions and doubts will vanish from the horizon, and you will look unto their place to find them gone. This indignant question is a question that the whole world asks, namely, 'What is the meaning of my life?'"

"In other words, these numbered years of our lives, which cost us so heavily, and the numerous pains and torments that we suffer for them to complete them to the fullest, who is it who enjoys them? Or even more precisely, whom do I delight?

"It is indeed true that historians have grown weary contemplating it, and particularly in our generation. No one even wishes to consider it.

"Yet the question stands as bitterly and as vehemently as ever. Sometimes it meets us uninvited, pecks at our minds and humiliates us to the ground before we find the famous ploy of flowing mindlessly in the currents of life as always."

(Baal HaSulam, "Introduction to the Study of the Ten Sefirot," Item 2)

**The wisdom of Kabbalah
is for anyone
who can no longer ignore the question
about the meaning of life.**

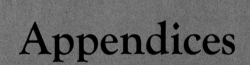

Appendices

An Interview with Dr. Michael Laitman

QUESTION: **What is most important to you in life?**

Answer: Dissemination of the correction method for the human ego in the world. The ego is the source of all that is evil in the world, and only its correction will bring happiness to the world.

QUESTION: **What is the essence of life?**

Answer: The essence of life for each person is his or her correction to the point of attaining the quality of love towards all of one's surroundings.

QUESTION: **What causes pedophilia, dissatisfaction, wars, terrorism, corruption, poverty, national and religious extremism, and why can no one defeat this evil?**

Answer: All the evil in the world is born out of people's egoistic nature. From the dawn of history the human ego has been incessantly growing and developing, driving humanity to develop society, to rule and to subjugate nature. We cannot restrain the ego by ourselves with our current means.

QUESTION: **What can save Earth from an ecological disaster?**

Answer: Only a shift in people's attitude toward the environment, meaning people and nature. We must shift from hatred and desire to exploit everything and everyone into giving and to an all-encompassing love.

A committee for saving Earth from human nature should be founded as soon as possible, with access to all the media. Through cooperation, it must teach humanity how to exist properly, mutually.

QUESTION: **How would you like to see the world and humanity?**

Answer: In the future, everyone will discover that they are elements that are completely interconnected and interdependent in a single system, as cogwheels in a machine. Every act and thought will stem from the complete mutual dependence that will be revealed, and this will force everyone to reach a common thought, plan, and action to change the world.

QUESTION: **What is your favorite saying?**

Answer: Life can exist only when all the elements are in complete harmony, as in a single, perfect body. The saying "Love thy neighbor as thyself" precisely embodies it. This saying does not refer to a desired moral level, but to the law that sustains life.

New Education for a New World

1. Globalization has turned into a factor that affects financial, political, and cultural development. It encompasses the international market, all social processes, and the lives of each and every one of us. However, it does not solve political, financial, social, cultural, or religious problems.

2. To help people adapt to the new reality, new education is required. Until now, education was established as part of the egoistic framework and separated world. The new education needs to come naturally, rather than result from nature's painful impact on us, forcing us to change the way we think, the relationships we form with each other, and to adjust them to the globalized reality.

Contrary to previous shifts we experienced throughout history, this time we are given an opportunity to execute the change by ourselves in a conscious manner, and not out of coercion.

3. Exchanging the regular culture for a global one needs to happen without force (the way we are accustomed to). For example, currently we force our children to study according to the old system, although they are already intended for a "new humanity." Our instinct is to suppress the new to which they naturally aspire.

4. Here, for the first time in history, the educational role of the media should manifest. Instead of being a dubious source of information, the media needs to gain trust by contributing to the education of the new generation. This is precisely the role of the media, followed by the educational institutions.

All the changes in society should start from the bottom. They must touch upon the standards of life, the moral principles, and the cultural-religious traditions. The new will not usurp the old, but rather develop naturally and painlessly by discovering the globalization of nature and society.

5. Kabbalistic education is not coercive, as there is no need to bring everyone to a uniform level of knowledge and culture. On the contrary, there is a place for all levels and cultures, since Kabbalistic education raises people above the different cultures, above conflicts, while enhancing the unity amongst them.

Every person may maintain his or her own religion, as Baal HaSulam writes in The Writings of the Last Generation. Kabbalistic education prevents conflicts and clashes between cultures, ideologies, and nations.

6. Although Kabbalah leads people to a common awareness, calling everyone to act as wheels within a single system, it does not belittle the role of the individual. Eventually, every person finds the right place in the mechanism, in the inclusive connection among all people, and realizes the full potential that nature has given him or her.

Through such an education, uniform principles of existence are created in the world. The individual awareness turns into group awareness, followed by the all-encompassing awareness of humanity. Furthermore, as Baal HaSulam writes, a blurring of boundaries will occur and a unified civilization will emerge.

The separation from sovereignty, the blurring of boundaries, and the formation of a single spiritual authority will not be done by coercion, but rather in accord with the awareness of the necessity of achieving equivalence of qualities with the Creator (the quality of love and bestowal).

Also, mass education can manifest through TV programs in addition to computer and internet games.

7. Globalization causes a feeling of density in the world. However, awareness of the uniformity of the system of souls turns the world into a warm and secure place.

Further Reading

Kabbalah for Beginners

Kabbalah for Beginners is a book for all those seeking answers to life's essential questions. We all want to know why we are here, why there is pain, and how we can make life more enjoyable. The four parts of this book provide us with reliable answers to these questions, as well as clear explanations of the gist of Kabbalah and its practical implementations.

Part One discusses the discovery of the wisdom of Kabbalah, and how it was developed, and finally concealed until our time. Part Two introduces the gist of the wisdom of Kabbalah, using ten easy drawings to help us understand the structure of the spiritual worlds, and how they relate to our world. Part Three reveals Kabbalistic concepts that are largely unknown to the public, and Part Four elaborates on practical means you and I can take, to make our lives better and more enjoyable for us and for our children.

Kabbalah Revealed

This is the most clearly written, reader-friendly guide to making sense of the surrounding world. Each of its six chapters focuses on a different aspect of the wisdom of Kabbalah, illuminating its teachings and explaining them using various examples from our day-to-day lives.

The first three chapters in *Kabbalah Revealed* explain why the world is in a state of crisis, how our growing desires promote progress as well as alienation, and why the biggest deterrent to achieving positive change is rooted in our own spirits. Chapters Four through Six offer a prescription for positive change. In these chapters, we learn how we can use our spirits to build a personally peaceful life in harmony with all of Creation.

Wondrous Wisdom

This book offers an initial course on Kabbalah. Like all the books presented here, *Wondrous Wisdom* is based solely on authentic teachings passed down from Kabbalist teacher to student over thousands of years. At the heart of the book is a sequence of lessons revealing the nature of Kabbalah's wisdom and explaining how to attain it. For every person questioning "Who am I really?" and "Why am I on this planet?" this book is a must.

Awakening to Kabbalah

A distinctive, personal, and awe-filled introduction to an ancient wisdom tradition. In this book, Michael Laitman offers a deeper understanding of the fundamental teachings of Kabbalah, and how you can use its wisdom to clarify your relationship with others and the world around you.

Using language both scientific and poetic, he probes the most profound questions of spirituality and existence. This provocative, unique guide will inspire and invigorate you to see beyond the world as it is and the limitations of your everyday life, become closer to the Creator, and reach new depths of the soul.

Kabbalah, Science, and the Meaning of Life

Science explains the mechanisms that sustain life; Kabbalah explains why life exists. In *Kabbalah, Science, and the Meaning of Life*, Michael Laitman combines science and spirituality in a captivating dialogue that reveals life's meaning.

For thousands of years Kabbalists have been writing that the world is a single entity divided into separate beings. Today the cutting-edge science of quantum physics states a very similar idea: that at the most fundamental level of matter, we are all literally one.

Science proves that reality is affected by the observer who examines it; and so does Kabbalah. But Kabbalah makes an even bolder statement: even the Creator, the Maker of reality, is within the observer. In other words, God is inside of us; He doesn't exist anywhere else. When we pass away, so does He.

These earthshaking concepts and more are eloquently introduced so that even readers new to Kabbalah or science will easily understand them. Therefore, if you're just a little curious about why you are here, what life means, and what you can do to enjoy it more, this book is for you.

From Chaos to Harmony

Many researchers and scientists agree that the ego is the reason behind the perilous state our world is in today. Laitman's groundbreaking book not only demonstrates that egoism has been the basis for all suffering throughout human history, but also shows how we can turn our plight to pleasure.

The book contains a clear analysis of the human soul and its problems, and provides a "roadmap" of what we need to do to once again be happy. *From Chaos to Harmony* explains how we can rise to a new level of existence on personal, social, national, and international levels.

Attaining the Worlds Beyond

From the introduction to *Attaining the Worlds Beyond*: "… Not feeling well on the Jewish New Year's Eve of September 1991, my teacher called me to his bedside and handed me his notebook, saying, 'Take it and learn from it.' The following morning, he perished in my arms, leaving me and many of his other disciples without guidance in this world.

"He used to say, 'I want to teach you to turn to the Creator, rather than to me, because He is the only strength, the only Source of all that exists, the only one who can really help you, and He awaits your prayers for help. When you seek help in your search for freedom from the bondage of this world, help in elevating yourself above this world, help in finding the self, and help in determining your purpose in life, you must turn to the Creator, who sends you all those aspirations in order to compel you to turn to Him.'"

Attaining the Worlds Beyond holds within it the content of that notebook, as well as other inspiring texts. This book reaches out to all those seekers who want to find a logical, reliable way to understand the world's phenomena. This fascinating introduction to the wisdom of Kabbalah will enlighten the mind, invigorate the heart, and move readers to the depths of their souls.

About Bnei Baruch

B nei Baruch is an international group of Kabbalists who share the wisdom of Kabbalah with the entire world. The study materials (in over 30 languages) are authentic Kabbalah texts that were passed down from generation to generation.

History and Origin

In 1991, following the passing of his teacher, Rav Baruch Shalom HaLevi Ashlag (The Rabash), Michael Laitman, Professor of Ontology and the Theory of Knowledge, PhD in Philosophy and Kabbalah, and MSc in Medical Bio-Cybernetics, established a Kabbalah study group called "Bnei Baruch." He called it Bnei Baruch (Sons of Baruch) to commemorate his mentor, whose side he never left in the final twelve years of his life, from 1979 to 1991. Dr. Laitman had been Ashlag's prime student and personal assistant, and is recognized as the successor to Rabash's teaching method.

The Rabash was the firstborn son and successor of Rav Yehuda Leib HaLevi Ashlag, the greatest Kabbalist of the 20th century. Rav Ashlag authored the most authoritative and comprehensive commentary on *The Book of Zohar*, titled The *Sulam* (Ladder) Commentary. He was the first to reveal the complete method for spiritual ascent, and thus was known as Baal HaSulam (Owner of the Ladder).

Bnei Baruch bases its entire study method on the path paved by these two great spiritual leaders.

The Study Method

The unique study method developed by Baal HaSulam and his son, the Rabash, is taught and applied on a daily basis by Bnei Baruch. This method relies on authentic Kabbalah sources such as *The Book of Zohar*, by Rabbi Shimon Bar-Yochai, *The Tree of Life*, by the Ari, and *The Study of the Ten Sefirot*, by Baal HaSulam.

While the study relies on authentic Kabbalah sources, it is carried out in simple language and uses a scientific, contemporary approach. The unique combination of an academic study method and personal experiences broadens the students' perspective and awards them a new perception of the reality they live in. Those on the spiritual path are thus given the necessary tools to study themselves and their surrounding reality.

Bnei Baruch is a diverse movement of tens of thousands of students worldwide. Students can choose their own paths and intensity of their studies according to their unique conditions and abilities.

The Message

The essence of the message disseminated by Bnei Baruch is universal: unity of the people, unity of nations and love of man.

For millennia, Kabbalists have been teaching that love of man should be the foundation of all human relations. This love prevailed in the days of Abraham, Moses, and the group of Kabbalists that they established. If we make room for these seasoned, yet contemporary values, we will discover that we possess the power to put differences aside and unite.

The wisdom of Kabbalah, hidden for millennia, has been waiting for the time when we would be sufficiently developed and ready to implement its message. Now, it is emerging as a solution that can unite diverse factions everywhere, enabling us, as individuals and as a society, to meet today's challenges.

Activities

Bnei Baruch was established on the premise that "only by expansion of the wisdom of Kabbalah to the public can we be awarded complete redemption" (Baal HaSulam). Therefore, Bnei Baruch offers a variety of ways for people to explore and discover the purpose of their lives, providing careful guidance for beginners and advanced students alike.

Internet
Bnei Baruch's international website, www.kab.info, presents the authentic wisdom of Kabbalah using essays, books, and original texts. It is by far the most expansive source of authentic Kabbalah material on the Internet, containing a unique, extensive library for readers to thoroughly explore the wisdom of Kabbalah. Additionally, the media archive, www.kabbalahmedia.info, contains thousands of media items, downloadable books, and a vast reservoir of texts, video and audio files in many languages.

Bnei Baruch's online Learning Center offers free Kabbalah courses for beginners, initiating students into this profound body of knowledge in the comfort of their own homes.

Dr. Laitman's daily lessons are also aired live on www.kab.tv, along with complementary texts and diagrams.

All these services are provided free of charge.

Television
In Israel, Bnei Baruch established its own channel, no. 66 on both cable and satellite, which broadcasts 24/7 Kabbalah

TV. The channel is also aired on the Internet at www.kab.tv. All broadcasts on the channel are free of charge. Programs are adapted for all levels, from complete beginners to the most advanced.

Conferences

Twice a year, students gather for a weekend of study and socializing at conferences in various locations in the U.S., as well as an annual convention in Israel. These gatherings provide a great setting for meeting like-minded people, for bonding, and for expanding one's understanding of the wisdom.

Kabbalah Books

Bnei Baruch publishes authentic books, written by Baal HaSulam, his son, the Rabash, as well as books by Dr. Michael Laitman. The books of Rav Ashlag and Rabash are essential for complete understanding of the teachings of authentic Kabbalah, explained in Laitman's lessons.

Dr. Laitman writes his books in a clear, contemporary style based on the key concepts of Baal HaSulam. These books are a vital link between today's readers and the original texts. All the books are available for sale, as well as for free download.

Paper

Kabbalah Today is a free paper produced and disseminated by Bnei Baruch in many languages, including English, Hebrew, Spanish, and Russian. It is apolitical, non-commercial, and written in a clear, contemporary style. The purpose of Kabbalah Today is to expose the vast knowledge hidden in the wisdom of Kabbalah at no cost and in a clear, engaging style for readers everywhere.

Kabbalah Lessons

As Kabbalists have been doing for centuries, Laitman gives a daily lesson. The lessons are given in Hebrew and are simultaneously interpreted into seven languages—English, Russian, Spanish, French, German, Italian, and Turkish—by skilled and experienced interpreters. As with everything else, the live broadcast is free of charge.

Funding

Bnei Baruch is a non-profit organization for teaching and sharing the wisdom of Kabbalah. To maintain its independence and purity of intentions, Bnei Baruch is not supported, funded, or otherwise tied to any government or political organization.

Since the bulk of its activity is provided free of charge, the prime sources of funding for the group's activities are donations and tithing—contributed by students on a voluntary basis—and Dr. Laitman's books, which are sold at cost.

Detailed Table of Contents

How to contact Bnei Baruch

1057 Steeles Avenue West,
Suite 532Toronto,
ON, M2R 3X1Canada

Bnei Baruch USA,
2009 85th street, #51,
Brooklyn, NY 11214, USA

E-mail: info@kabbalah.info

Web site: www.kab.info

Toll free in USA and Canada:
1-866-LAITMAN
Fax: 1-905 886 9697